The Story of the

SCOTLAND

National Team

Foreword

Football is Scotland's most popular sport and the national team has always meant so much to so many Scots.

Our fans, 'The Tartan Army', have a superb reputation around the world for their passion and ability to make friends.

The first official international match took place in Glasgow between Scotland and England way back in 1872 – it ended 0–0 that day, but over the years the Scots have enjoyed victories over many of the game's superpowers, including Italy, Germany, France and the Netherlands.

Scotland have taken part in eight World Cups and two European Championships and produced many top class players, such as Kenny Dalglish, Denis Law and Jim Baxter – and who can forget James McFadden's wonder goal to beat France in Paris!

I hope young Scotland fans enjoy reading about the highs and lows of Scottish football through *The Story of the Scotland National Team* as much as I did.

Alex Salmond
First Minister of Scotland

6

Just before two o'clock on 30 November, 1872, 11 proud Englishmen ran out onto a cricket pitch in Partick, Glasgow.

They were there not to play cricket but to show the Scots how to play a newer game they had invented, called 'association football'.

On the Scottish side were 11 players from the country's biggest team, Queen's Park. 4,000 curious spectators came along to watch.

The St Andrew's Day fixture ended in a 0–0 draw, and would go down in history as the first ever international football match.

As the 0–0 scoreline shows, the Scottish side was stronger than the English team expected. In fact, even though the English had written the rules to association football and thought of it as 'their' game, it spread through Scotland like wildfire …

INTERNATIONAL
FOOT-BALL MATCH,
(ASSOCIATION RULES,)
ENGLAND v. SCOTLAND,
WEST OF SCOTLAND CRICKET GROUND
HAMILTON CRESCENT, PARTICK,
SATURDAY, 30th November, 1872, at 2 p.m.
———
ADMISSION—ONE SHILLING
No. 806

Not only was the game instantly popular in Scotland, the Scots quickly became much better at it than their southern neighbours.

So much better that, of the 19 Scotland v England matches between 1872 and 1890, the Scots won 11, drew five and lost only three.

This might seem surprising, but it was really very simple. The English may have invented association football, but the Scots had come up with an even better invention: **passing** football.

The English idea of football was that a player would dribble the ball as far upfield as he could before shooting at goal or being tackled.

The rest of the team followed up in a 'pack' and tried to pounce on the loose ball so that the charge could start all over again.

But the clever Scots realised that it was much better to pass the ball to a team-mate **before** being tackled, then run forward to receive a return pass.

SCOTCH PROFESSORS HAND ENGLISH A FOOTBALL LESSON

BOYS IN BLUE FIND WINNING FORMULA WITH NEW "PASSING STYLE"

They became so good at this passing and running game that English teams soon began recruiting Scottish players to teach them how to do it.

These men were nicknamed 'the Scotch professors' because they played the game in a 'scientific' way.

At this time English teams were allowed to pay their players so many Scotch professors crossed the border.

At first these 'Anglo-Scots' were seen as traitors by people in Scotland.

The Scottish Football Association (SFA), which had been set up in 1873, would not allow the Anglos to play for Scotland.

But in 1896, after six years without a win over England, the SFA realised that they would have to change their tune.

They organised a trial match for the Anglos and five of them made it into the Scotland team for that year's match against England. Scotland won 2–1.

ANDREW WATSON

In 1881 a young defender called Andrew Watson made his debut for Scotland – and went down in history. Not only did Andrew captain the national side to a thrilling 6-1 win over England, he became the first black footballer to play international football.

Andrew was from British Guyana, a part of South America which was ruled by Britain at that time. His father was a Scottish sugar farmer, and his mother a local Guyanan girl.

Andrew was sent to school in England and then went to Glasgow University.

He started playing for Queen's Park, and was so good that he was selected for the national team.

Andrew played three times for Scotland but in 1882 he moved to England, which meant that the SFA would no longer pick him to play for Scotland.

Andrew Watson is pictured in the 'Rosebery colours'.
Early Scotland teams sometimes wore the primrose-and-pink racing colours of the SFA president, Lord Rosebery.

It was not just Scotland and England who were going football crazy. The game quickly spread to Wales and Ireland too.

Like England, Wales and Ireland were no match for the super Scots in the early years. Scotland hammered the Welsh 4–0 in their first meeting in 1876, and won the next 12 matches against their Celtic cousins.

The first clash with Ireland came in 1884 and Scotland did not lose a single match against them until 1903.

By the start of the 20th century football was by far the most popular sport in Scotland. A crowd of 63,000 turned up to watch the national team beat England 4–1 in 1900, and six years later there were 102,741 people crammed inside Hampden for the same fixture.

HAMPDEN

The present home of Queen's Park and the national team was built in 1903, and was the third ground to have the name of Hampden Park.

At the time it was the most modern football stadium in the world – the first to have turnstiles, a public address system and a car park.

Until 1950, when the Maracana was built in Brazil, Hampden was also the world's largest sports stadium. It still holds the record for the biggest crowd in the history of European football – 149,415 for a Scotland v England match in 1937.

The noise made by such enormous crowds could be heard for miles around, and became known as the Hampden Roar.

The powerful men in charge of football liked the money that these crowds brought in, but no one thought too much about their safety.

It was only a matter of time before tragedy struck. Unfortunately it struck at a Scotland v England match.

In 1902 the Auld Enemies met at Ibrox Stadium, home of Rangers, because Hampden was being rebuilt.

Rangers had recently rebuilt **their** ground but 10 minutes into the match part of the wooden terracing collapsed, creating a gaping hole.

Hundreds of supporters plummeted through the hole and hit the ground 40 feet below. Twenty-six died and around 500 were injured.

Incredibly, the match continued after a 30-minute break and ended in a 1–1 draw.

People were shocked by the 'Ibrox disaster' but it did not stop them going to watch football – and Scotland v England games continued to attract massive crowds.

England had copied Scotland's pass-and-move style, and started to challenge the Scots strongly. In the early decades of the 20th century the games were usually closely fought.

This made the events of 31 March, 1928 all the more astonishing …

WEMBLEY WIZARDS

On 31 March, 1928 Scotland became the first team to beat England at their Wembley home.

And the Scots did not just beat the English, they tore them apart – winning by five goals to one.

The 11 Scotsmen who played that day will be remembered forever as the Wembley Wizards.

They were:

John Harkness (Queen's Park), *James Nelson* (Cardiff City), *Thomas Law* (Chelsea), *Jimmy Gibson* (Aston Villa), *Thomas Bradshaw* (Bury), *Jimmy McMullan* (Man City, capt), *Alex Jackson* (Huddersfield), *James Dunn* (Hibs), *Hughie Gallacher* (Newcastle), *Alec James* (Preston), *Alan Morton* (Rangers)

Scorers: Jackson (2, 44 & 65 mins), *James* (67 & 85 mins)

As the Auld Enemies lined up at Wembley in that year's Home Championship match, England were the strong favourites. Many people thought the Scotland forward line was too small. Of the five attackers, only one stood over 5ft 6in tall!

The Scots might have been small in height but they were big in heart, and played England off the park.

Alex Jackson grabbed a hat-trick as the Wembley Wizards thrashed their neighbours 5–1.

Football had spread to Europe and South America around the turn of the century, and FIFA was set up in 1904 to control football all over the world.

But the home nations of Scotland, England, Wales and Ireland did not join at first because FIFA thought Britain should have one place, not four. This wasn't the last argument with FIFA …

In 1930 FIFA decided to organise a brand new tournament, to be held every four years. They decided to call the new event the World Cup.

The first competition took place in Uruguay, in South America – but the SFA had fallen out with FIFA again so Scotland did not play. In the early years of the World Cup Scotland were not very interested – how things have changed!

FOOTBALL

SCOTTISH TEAM ARRIVES AT CALAIS

CALAIS, Friday

The Scottish Association football team which is to meet France in Paris on Sunday arrived here to-day after an excellent crossing. Campbell (Airdrieonians), the captain, confirmed the fact that Hill would play left, half-back instead of W. S. King. "With our excellent forward line we expect to beat France," said Campbell. The team will not have any practice in Paris before the match – P.A. Foreign Special.

SCOTLAND VICTORIOUS AT PARIS

GALLACHER'S TWO GOALS

France, 0; Scotland, 2

PARIS, Sunday

In fine weather and before a large attendance, Scotland beat France in an Association football match by two goals to none at the Colombes Stadium here to-day. Both Scotland's goals were scored by Gallacher, one in each half.

After a short period of Scottish pressure the Frenchmen showed that however inaccurate their passing was they were nimble, and the Scottish goal underwent a few moments of justifiable anxiety. But Thomson saved with the whole French forward line massed in front of his goal.

A movement on the Scottish left carried play to the other end, and the French goal-keeper was applauded for three fine saves in rapid succession.

So the only games against teams from beyond the British Isles were friendlies. One of Scotland's first matches on foreign soil was played against France in Paris in 1930 and the Scots won 2–0.

Another 24 years would pass before Scotland finally took part in the World Cup finals.

They had actually made it through to the 1950 finals but decided not to take part. They did not think it would be proper for runners-up to go to the finals in Brazil and turned down the invitation.

So Switzerland 1954 was to be Scotland's first taste of a World Cup finals.

They were to discover that, while they had been concentrating on matches against the home nations, the football skills of the Europeans and South Americans had been coming on leaps and bounds.

In Switzerland, things started to go wrong even before the tournament had begun. The Scots were so badly prepared that they did not even have a training kit, and had to train in their own club jerseys. Because of this they were nicknamed 'the liquorice allsorts'.

Three important players – including giant defender George Young – were allowed to go on tour with their club, Rangers, instead of representing their country.

Even with a full-strength team the Scots would have struggled. In the group stages they were up against defending champions Uruguay and the experienced Austrians.

Scotland put up a brave fight against the Austrians, losing 1–0. But the Uruguay match was a disaster. First, Scotland manager Andy Beattie resigned … and then the sun came out.

It was one of the hottest days of the year and the Scotland players were wearing their thick winter jerseys. They wilted in the heat and were hammered 7–0.

The next World Cup was to be held in Sweden in 1958.

For the first time the home nations were placed in different qualifying groups. And, for the first and last time, they all made it!

Just like in 1954, Scotland suffered a cruel blow in the lead-up to the big event. Manchester United's Matt Busby – one of the greatest managers of all time – had agreed to lead the national team to Sweden but was seriously injured in an air crash in Munich that killed eight United players.

QUALIFYING GROUP TABLE

UEFA Group 9

10 Mar 1957	Madrid	Spain 2–2 Switzerland
08 May 1957	Glasgow	Scotland 4–2 Spain
19 May 1957	Basel	Switzerland 1–2 Scotland
26 May 1957	Madrid	Spain 4–1 Scotland
06 Nov 1957	Glasgow	Scotland 3–2 Switzerland
24 Nov 1957	Lausanne	Switzerland 1–4 Spain

	P	W	D	L	Gls	Pts
Scotland	4	3	0	1	10-9	6
Spain	4	2	1	1	12-8	5
Switzerland	4	0	1	3	6-11	1

So the Scotland team went to Sweden without Matt. They started well with a draw against Yugoslavia – their first point in a World Cup finals – but lost to Paraguay and France to have their hopes dashed again.

They would have to wait 16 long years before getting a chance to make amends …

With no World Cup finals to look forward to, Scottish fans were desperate for success against the home nations – and especially against England.

So when the Scots were thrashed 9–3 at Wembley in 1961, the whole country was saddened and embarrassed. Scotland's goalkeeper that day, Frank Haffey, was so upset he went to live in Australia!

WEMBLEY 1-2-3-4-5-6-7-8-9!

OUR BLACKEST HOUR

The rout begins

MID-WEEK GAMES

The pain was eased two years later as Jim Baxter scored twice in a famous 2–1 victory. And things got even better on an amazing April day at Wembley in 1967 …

England had won the World Cup just nine months before, and were still unbeaten when Scotland came to play.

Alf Ramsay's all-conquering team thought the Scots would be pushovers.

How wrong they were.

Not only did Scotland beat England, they ran rings around them.

The Scotland scorers were Denis Law, Bobby Lennox and Jim McCalliog but the real star of the show was Rangers midfielder Jim Baxter.

Jim tortured the English defence all afternoon, and even played keepy-uppy as he waited for his opponents to come and tackle him!

The final score of 3–2 made the match look close but even the English team admitted that Scotland's new Wembley Wizards had played them off the park.

Scotland were the unofficial World Champions!

By the time Scotland booked their passage to Germany 74 the World Cup finals had grown into the biggest sporting event on the planet.

For the first time the Scotland manager, Willie Ormond, had been allowed to pick his own squad. Up until then the players had been chosen by a group of selectors.

Willie's boys got off to a good start, beating Zaire 2–0 with goals from Peter Lorimer and Joe Jordan. It was Scotland's first win in a World Cup finals, but they missed chances to score more goals. Those misses would come back to haunt them.

After little Zaire, Scotland took on the mighty Brazil – the world champions.

They came away with a point – but were just two inches from a famous victory. Billy Bremner was right in front of the Brazilian goal when he got his foot to a rebound but the ball trickled agonisingly past the post.

Scotland drew 1–1 with Yugoslavia in their last group match, which meant that their hopes of qualifying for the knockout stages rested on the Brazil v Zaire match.

As the Scots players walked off the park they were given the heartbreaking news that Brazil had won 3-0, meaning that Brazil and Yugoslavia would go through. For the first, but not the last time, Scotland were knocked out on goal difference and had to pack their bags early.

SCOTLAND'S WORLD CUP RECORD

Scotland have qualified for the World Cup finals nine times – but have only gone to eight of them. This is because they thought it would be wrong to take part in 1950 as they did not win their qualifying group!

Between 1974 and 1990 Scotland qualified for five World Cups in a row. Unfortunately they have never managed to make it past the group stage of the competition... yet.

SCOTLAND'S WORLD CUPS

Year	Country	Managers
1954	Switzerland	Andy Beattie
1958	Sweden	Matt Busby/Dawson Walker
1974	Germany	Willie Ormond
1978	Argentina	Ally MacLeod
1982	Spain	Jock Stein
1986	Mexico	Alex Ferguson
1990	Italy	Andy Roxburgh
1998	France	Craig Brown

The 1978 World Cup finals were to be held in Argentina but Scotland faced a tricky qualifying group that included Wales and European champions, Czechoslovakia.

In the end it came down to a do-or-die final match against the Welsh. So many people wanted tickets that the game was switched to Liverpool's ground, Anfield, which was much bigger than Wales' home ground, Ninian Park.

That proved to be a bad move for the Welsh – because Scotland's Tartan Army snapped up 30,000 of the 50,000 tickets and roared their team to a 2–0 win. Next stop, Argentina …

With great players like Kenny Dalglish, Joe Jordan and Archie Gemmill in the squad, the whole country was sure that this would be the most successful World Cup so far.

Scotland's manager, Ally MacLeod, was in no mood to dampen down the nation's hopes. In fact, he even suggested that his team might win the whole tournament!

The fans were so excited that 30,000 of them turned up at Hampden Park to see the squad off. Scotland was on the march with Ally's Army and the support really did believe that the players would bring the World Cup back from South America.

In Argentina, though, things started badly… and got worse. Scotland lost their first game 3–1 to Peru. Then winger Willie Johnston failed a drugs test, and was sent home in disgrace.

There was even more disappointment when Ally MacLeod's men drew with Iran. This meant the Scots had to beat the mighty Holland by three goals to go through to the knockout stages.

Scotland raced into a 2–1 lead then Archie Gemmill gave the fans a magic moment that they still talk about today …

Archie picked the ball up on the right wing and zig-zagged past three Dutch defenders before calmly lifting the ball over keeper Jan Jongbloed. Even the Holland fans in the stadium clapped for Archie, because they realised they had just seen one of the best World Cup goals of all time.

Suddenly the dream was back on – but Holland scored again to send Scotland home before the knockout rounds once again.

In 1982, Scotland qualified for the World Cup for the third time in a row and once again they faced the mighty Brazil. Davie Narey scored with a famous 'toe-poke' to give the Scots a shock lead but that only made the Brazilians angry and they went on to crush Scotland 4–1.

For the third time in a row they were eliminated on goal difference – despite being led by the great Jock Stein.

Big Jock remained in charge after Spain 82, and by September 1985 he had guided his team to the brink of qualification for Mexico 86.

All they needed was a point against Wales in Cardiff.

Scotland got their point, but Big Jock paid the highest price possible. With the Scots trailing 1–0 in the second half Jock decided to send on Davie Cooper. It was the right decision, but it was also to be Jock's last.

Davie equalised with an 81st minute penalty but as the players and fans celebrated the manager collapsed in the dug-out.

It was a heart attack. Doctors tried their best to save Big Jock but he died on the treatment table of the away dressing room.

When the fans heard the news, their cheers turned to tears as they realised they had lost one of the greatest managers of all time.

The job of taking Scotland to Mexico was given to a bright young manager called Alex Ferguson. Alex had enjoyed great success with Aberdeen and was about to join Manchester United.

However he could not work his magic with Scotland, and they came home from Mexico with only one point from three matches.

In 1990 in Italy, Scotland made it a double 'five-in-a-row'. The national team, managed by Andy Roxburgh, qualified for the World Cup finals for the fifth time on the trot. And they were put out before the group stages for the fifth time on the trot, too.

But the Scots fans who followed their heroes to Italy were left with some wonderful memories – especially of the day Scotland played Sweden in Genoa.

Not only did the team win 2–1, with goals from Stuart McCall and Mo Johnston, the Tartan Army also won many friends that night – marching to the stadium with the Swedish supporters and showing the world how football fans **should** behave.

From that day on, the Tartan Army became famous for winning friends and admirers wherever they went.

THE TARTAN ARMY

Scotland's supporters are known as the Tartan Army – because they dress in kilts, which usually have a criss-crossed tartan pattern.

The Tartan Army are known all over the world for their passionate support but also for their friendliness and sense of fun.

They are Scotland's 12th man when they pack into Hampden for home matches. And they also travel in large numbers to support the team abroad.

People living in foreign cities are often amazed by the sight of thousands of Tartan Army 'foot soldiers' marching from the town centre to the stadium!

They only had to wait two years before meeting up with their new Swedish friends again – because in 1992 Scotland qualified for their first European Championship finals, to be held in Sweden.

The draw was unkind to Andy Roxburgh's team. They would be up against Germany, Holland and Russia (who were called CIS at that time).

Scotland lost narrowly to Holland and Germany. Once again they were heading home early, but they went out on a high with a 3–0 win over Russia, with goals from Paul McStay, Brian McClair and Gary McAllister.

Even though they had ignored them at first, Scotland's football bosses and supporters now saw the World Cup and European Championships as the most important events.

The home internationals, which for so long meant so much to fans, had been abandoned in 1984. And even the oldest international fixture in the world, Scotland v England, had been stopped in 1989.

But that did not mean that the Auld Enemies would never meet again. In fact, they only had to wait seven years for another chance to settle old scores.

The 1996 European Championships took place in England, and there were gasps when the draw was made – because Scotland were placed in the same group as their hosts, and would take them on at Wembley once again.

So, on June 15, 1996, the two teams took the field with 76,000 fans packed into England's national stadium.

Alan Shearer put England ahead but Scotland came back strongly and won a penalty with 12 minutes to go.

Gary McAllister stepped up to take the kick but England goalkeeper David Seaman saved Gary's effort. To make matters worse for Scotland, England raced up the other end of the pitch and gave the ball to Paul Gascoigne.

'Gazza' scored one of the best goals ever by flicking the ball over Colin Hendry's head and volleying it into the net.

Scotland still had a chance to qualify for the knockout stage but, despite a 1–0 win over Switzerland, they were unlucky to go out on goal difference yet again.

Two years later Craig Brown's Scotland qualified for the World Cup in France.

Little did they know that it would be their last… so far.

The eyes of the world were on Scotland as they faced Brazil in the opening match of the tournament. The game started badly when Brazil scored an early goal but the Scots fought back and won a penalty. John Collins stepped up to take it – and was so cool under pressure that he cracked a smile as he stroked the ball home!

It was not to be Scotland's day, though, and an unlucky Tom Boyd own goal 14 minutes from the end gave Brazil a 2–1 victory.

Scotland then played well in a 1–1 draw with Norway but the tournament ended in bitter disappointment when the Scots were hammered 3–0 by Morocco in their final group match.

After failing to qualify for the European Championships of 2000 and the World Cup of 2002, Craig Brown was replaced as Scotland coach by Berti Vogts.

Berti was from Germany and had won the World Cup as a player in 1974 and the European Championships as Germany manager in 1996.

But Berti had a tough time as Scotland manager, and his team missed out on Euro 2004 and the 2006 World Cup.

The players and supporters were downhearted and wondered whether their national team could ever become a force to be reckoned with once again.

Happily, the answer was 'yes'.

Walter Smith, who had enjoyed success as a manager with Rangers and Everton, took over from Berti.

His first big task was to try to qualify for Euro 2008, but when Scotland were drawn in the same group as France, Italy and Ukraine, everyone said it was mission impossible.

But Walter's boys beat France at Hampden to put themselves in a good position. Then Walter left to go back to Rangers and Alex McLeish took over.

Alex continued Walter's good work by leading his boys to an amazing 1–0 win over France in Paris – with James McFadden scoring one of the greatest Scotland goals of all time.

In the end Scotland's destiny came down to their final match, where they took on Italy at Hampden. It was very simple: if they beat the Italians, Scotland were on their way to Euro 2008.

Sadly, Alex's bravehearts could not perform the miracle and lost 2–1 to a last-minute goal from the World Champions.

Alex McLeish then stepped down as manager to take over at Birmingham.

He was replaced by George Burley, a former Scotland player who had been manager of Ipswich, Derby, Hearts and Southampton.

Now George has the task of steering Scotland to the 2010 World Cup finals in South Africa.

With Holland and Norway in their qualifying group, it will not be easy. But with the Tartan Army roaring them on, nothing is impossible for George and his boys.